100+ SUPER PIG JOKES, PUNS, AND RIDDLES

SCHOLASTIC INC.
New York Toronto London Auckland Sydney

100+ SUPER PIG JOKES, PUNS, AND RIDDLES

Shirley and Cherie Parenteau

Illustrated by
TONY TALLARICO

SCHOLASTIC INC.
New York Toronto London Auckland Sydney

To Dad and Scott for listening.

ISBN 0-590-41656-1

12 11 10 9 8 7 6 5 4   1 2/9

Printed in the U.S.A.   01

Introduction

When Cherie Parenteau's cute piglets grew into hogs, she began collecting pigs of other kinds. Now a teenager, she has over two hundred pigs of many materials — and a trough full of pig jokes and riddles. She's penned the best for this book.

Printed in the U.S.A.

Why isn't there a Superpig?
It's too hard for a pig to change clothes in
a telephone booth.

What did the pig say when it found a fly in its soup?
"Yum Yum."

* * *

How did the little pig win at Monopoly?
He built hotels on Pork Place.

* * *

Where do bad pigs go?
They get sent to the pen.

* * *

ANSWERS THE 3 LITTLE PIGS DIDN'T GIVE THE WOLF:
"You've got the wrong house. Red's Grandma lives next door."
"Nobody's home. *All* the little piggies went to market."
"Have you cleared this for environmental impact?"

Where did the piglets study their ABC's?
At a school for higher loining.

* * *

Farmer Jones is so interested in conserving energy, he built a pig-powered car.

He has to get rid of it, though. Every time he turns a corner, the tires squeal.

Have you heard about the pig who took up disco dancing?

He liked to swing his weight around.

Did you hear the story about the razorback hog?
It's pretty dull.

* * *

Why can't there be a Santa Pig?

Pigs don't fit in chimneys.

What do little pigs want to be when they grow up?

Garbage collectors.

Why did the little pig hide the soap?
He heard the farmer yell, "Hogwash!"

Call common to ambulance-chasing pigs:
"SUE-EEEE!"

Why did the pigs rush to the space center?
They heard it was launch (lunch) time.

TEACHER: If it took six pigs two hours to eat
the apples in the orchard, how
many hours would it take three
pigs?
SUZY FARMER: None, because the six pigs
have already eaten them all.

**Why do pigs go to New York City?
To see The Big Apple.**

How do they get there?
In pigup trucks.

What are they warned to look out for?
Pigpockets.

Where do pigs meet when they get to New York?
In Central Pork.

Then where do they go?
To Madison Square Garden, but they're always disappointed.

Why are pigs disappointed with Madison Square Garden?
They can never find the vegetables.

***

Why did the pig wear yellow coveralls?

r-r-r-rip!

He split a seam in his blue ones.

* * *

WOLF: Knock! Knock!
LITTLE PIG: Who's there?
WOLF: Beth.
LITTLE PIG: Beth who?
WOLF: Beth let me in or I'll blow your howth down!

FARMER: What's that pig doing in the middle of the road with a red light on its head?

FARMER'S HELPER: Didn't you tell me to put out a stop swine?

11

Why are pigs such great football fans?
They're always rooting.

Why did the piglets get in trouble in their stained glass class?
They stained it with mud.

Why did the piglets get in trouble in their biology class?
They ate all the specimens.

Why wouldn't the sow let her piglets play with toads?
She didn't want them to grow into wart hogs.

CITY COUSIN: Pigs don't look very smart to me.
COUNTRY KID: Sure, they are. You ever see a sow try to make a silk purse out of a farmer's ear?

Why did the spotted pigs run away?

They thought the traveling salesman told the farmer to put his name on the dotted swine.

Why did the little pig try to join the Navy?
He loved to sing, "Oinkers Aweigh!"

FARMER: All our pigs are learning karate.
VISITOR: Oh, I don't believe that.
FARMER: No? Well, just watch out for their
        chops.

What did the pig do when a beetle landed in his feed trough?
He ate it quickly, before the others could ask him to share.

* * *

What do pigs like with chow mein?
Sooey sauce.

* * *

What did the pig say when he found a line of ants in his trough?
"Mmm. Canapes."

* * *

Why did he call the ants "canapes?"
He couldn't pronounce "hors d'oeuvres."

FIRST LITTLE PIG: How do you know your
boyfriend loves you?
SECOND LITTLE PIG: He always signs his
letters with lots of
hogs and kisses.

17

How does the pig farmer get to the fair?
He rides piggyback.

What song do pigs sing on New Year's Eve?
Auld Lang Swine.

Why did the piglets do badly in school?
They were all slow loiners.

Did you hear about the piglets who wanted to do something special for their mother's birthday?
No, what did they do?
They threw a sowprize party.

How does a pig write home?
With a pig pen.

FARMER'S WIFE: John! Our pigs have disappeared!
FARMER: Didn't I tell you not to put them on a diet?

Why doesn't Santa hitch his sleigh to a pig?
Pigs don't have red noses.

What soft drink do pigs like best?
Root beer.

Why couldn't the pig pay his bill?
He was a little shoat.

Is lunch the favorite subject of piglets?
No, it's theatre. They love to ham it up and
hog all the attention.

Why is the little pig mad at his brothers?
They're always squealing on him.

Did you hear about the pig who opened a pawn
shop?
He called it "Ham Hocks".

Did you hear about the pig who tried to start
a hot-air balloon business?
He couldn't get it off the ground.

What do you get when you cross a pig with
a canary?
I don't know, but when it sits on your electric
wire and sings, all your lights go out.

24

What did the mama pig say to her bad little
piglet?
"Behave or Frankenswine will get you."

Why did the pig author stop writing?
He ran out of oink.

Why was he happy when reviewers criticized his story?
Because they called it garbage.

VOICE: Knock! Knock!
LITTLE PIG: Who's there?
VOICE: Gladys.
LITTLE PIG: Gladys who?
VOICE: Gladys not me the wolf wants for
       dinner!

Why did he send it to New York?
He wanted to be published on Pork Avenue.

What famous pig actor made a movie about
Frankenswine?
Boaris Karloff.

What did he call his manuscript?
A shoat story.

★ ★ ★

What goes "knio, knio?"
A backward pig.

What kind of bread do pig ladies make in the Yukon?
Sow-r dough bread.

What kind of furniture do pigs like best?
Overstuffed.

Pig's explanation for the creation of the Universe:
The Pig Bang Theory.

When pigs get a toothache, who do they see?
Painless Porker.

The kids are crazy about a new piglet toy. When they wind it up, it eats all the spinach off their plates.

What do you say to a naked pig?
"I never sausage a body."

Why did the pig join the Army?
He heard the food was a mess.

Did you hear about the pig's vacation? They had a wonderful time at Yellowstone National Park. They dressed up as bears and raided all the garbage cans.

Is it true the pigs went over Niagara Falls in a barrel?
No, that story's just a lot of hogwash.

Why are there so many piggy banks?
Pigs don't like to hide their money in the mattress.

FARMER TO CITY GUEST: Did you sleep well last night?
GUEST: No, the bed was soft and the air was fresh, but an old sow kept pushing at the door.
FARMER: Never mind her. She always gets upset when we rent out her room.

Why wouldn't the piglet's mother let her read romantic novels?
She was afraid her daughter would run away with a wolf.

Why did the pigs paint their hoofs green?
It was Saint Patrick's Day.

Why did they wear green hats?
They were pretending to be leprechauns.

What was the name of the hog who was knighted by King Arthur?
Sir Lunchalot.

Why do pigs like February 14th?

They get lots of Valenswines.

Why do pigs love Halloween?

There's lots of hogsgobblin.

Where do city pigs live?
In sty-scrapers.

* * *

What do you call pigs in a demolition derby?
Crashing boars.

* * *

KNOCK! KNOCK!
WHO'S THERE?
OSWALD.
OSWALD WHO?
OSWALD THREE PIGS AND AH'M STILL
HUNGRY!

* * *

Did you hear of the pig who began hiding
garbage in November?
She wanted to do her Christmas slopping
early.

Why did the pig join a muscle-building class?
He thought "pumping iron" was a new juice dispenser.

Why do pigs have flat snouts?
From running in to trees.

Why do pigs run in to trees?
To shake out the alligators.

I've never seen an alligator in a tree.
That's because the pigs do such a good job.

Why should you never invite a pig to join your
tug-of-war team?
Pigs *want* to be pulled through the mudhole.

What do you call a pig who overacts?
A ham ham.

What do you call a pig with the flu?
A swine swine.

Two pigs robbed a bank. Why were they caught so quickly?

They squealed on each other.

The hog was a failure as a TV talk show host.
Why? What happened?
He turned out to be a big boar.

A city child came running into the farmhouse.
"No wonder that mama pig is so big," she
yelled. "There's a bunch of little pigs out there
blowing her up!"

Why did the farmer name his pig "Ink?"
Because it kept running out of the pen.

* * *

What is the pig's favorite musical instrument?
The piggalo (piccalo).

DEPIGNITIONS:
Illness most feared by pigs: Swine flu.
A tribe of tiny pigs: Pigmys.
A popular pig ballet: Swine Lake.
An Egyptian pig pharoah: Tut-Oink-Amen.
A tiny pig with wings: A Pigsy (pixy).

What did the pig say when the wolf grabbed her tail?
"That's the end of me!"

CITY COUSIN: I see you're getting ready for a big company dinner.
FARMER'S WIFE: What do you mean?
CITY COUSIN: I just passed the orchard and saw a pig with an apple in its mouth.

What happened to the pig who got a driver's license?
He became a road hog.

SONG HITS FROM THE PIGPEN:
"Pig O' My Heart"
"Swiney River"
"Oh, Sowzanna"
"Sooeet Sue"

Name the pig's favorite Shakespeare play.
Hamlet.

★ ★ ★

What did the fat pig say when the farmer
dumped corn mash into the trough?
"I'm afraid that's all going to waist."

★ ★ ★

What did the farmer say when his fat pig
wouldn't fit into the pen?
"There's more there than meets the sty."

★ ★ ★

Which side of a pig has the most bristles?
The outside.

What kind of pig do sows dislike?
Male Chauvinist Pigs.

What would a pig name a chain of food stores?
"Stop 'N Slop Markets"

What would happen if his employees went on strike?
They'd form pigget lines.

When is a pig an ecologist?
When he recycles garbage into ham.

What do you do for a pig with sore muscles?
Rub him with oinkment.

What do pigs do on nice afternoons?
They go on pignics.

What should you say to a pig on roller skates?

Don't say anything. Just get out of the way.

What did the mama pig say when junior pig bought a basket of wormy apples?

"Don't tell the farmer. He might charge us extra."

MOTHER PIG: What did you learn in school today?

FIRST LITTLE PIG: Oink! Oink!

SECOND LITTLE PIG: Oink! Oink!

THIRD LITTLE PIG: Arf! Arf!

MOTHER PIG: What!

THIRD LITTLE PIG: I'm taking a foreign language.

★ ★ ★

Farmer Jones bought a herd of pigs from a Roman farmer who moved into the next valley and boy, is he sorry. The hogs won't come to the feed trough unless he calls them in Pig Latin.

★ ★ ★

VOICE: Knock! Knock!

LITTLE PIG:: Who's there?

VOICE: Orange.

LITTLE PIG: Orange who?

VOICE: Orange you glad it's not the wolf?

What position does the pig play in football?

Loinback.

* * *

Why is a pig in a water trough like a penny?
Because its head is on one side and its tail is
on the other.

Why is he unhappy in the Minors?
Because he wants to play in the Pig Leagues.

Sports fad invented by pigs: Mud wrestling.

What do hip pigs call their ladies?
Fine swine.

How can you tell the pig is a failure as Easter
bunny?
By the egg on its face.

If an elephant is the symbol of the Republican Party and a donkey is the symbol of the Democratic Party, what is a pig the symbol of?

Any party where there's lots of food.

What did the pig say when his brother rolled on him?

"Heavy!"

CITY SMART ALEC: Why is your dad chasing those pigs through the garden?
SMARTER COUNTRY COUSIN: We're raising mashed potatoes.

★ ★ ★

Why didn't the pigs eat the rotten eggs in their feed trough?
They were saving the best for last.

★ ★ ★

Why wouldn't the bird let her chicks go near the pig pen?
She didn't want the pigs eating shredded tweet.

★ ★ ★

VISITOR: How do you get your pigs to sleep at night?
FARMER: No problem. Everyone here goes to bed with the chickens.
VISITOR: You must have a very large chicken house.

Why is the cook worried about catching his runaway pig?
He knows a little ham goes a long way.

BUMPER STICKERS FOR BIG PIGS:
Fat Is Where It's At!
Pig Power!
Honk If You're Obese!
A Mudbath A Day Keeps Sunburn Away!
I'd Rather Be Eating!

Why didn't the Bionic Pig get a TV series of
his own?
He made the mistake of going to a barbecue
with the Bionic Man and the Bionic Woman.

What do you call a pig with good table man-
ners?
Sick.

Did you hear about the pigs who took up
motorcycling?
They wanted to catch bugs with their teeth.

ANGRY FARMER TO HELPER: I told you not
to let those pigs in my office. Now, look what's
happened. They've eaten all the dates off my
calendar!

Why did the big pig want to go on stage?
There was a lot of ham in him.

Why did the little piglet fall in love with the hog?
Because he was such a sloppy dresser.

A pig's favorite movie: The Monster That Ate
New York.

How does Suzy Piglet's mother call her?
"Sue-ee! Sue-ee!"

When pigs have a party, who jumps out of the
cake?
Nobody. The pigs all jump in.

Why won't pigs take up jogging?
They don't like to get that far from the table.

How does a mama pig put her piglets to sleep?
She reads them pig tales.

**Which of these jokes do the pigs like best?
The corniest ones.**

What do you call a lady pig planting seeds?
A sow sow.

If you drop this book in a pig pen, what should
you do?
Take the words out of their mouths.

Farmer Brown put up a pig-shaped weather
vane, but he's not happy with it. Instead of
pointing with the wind, the pig vane keeps
pointing toward the feed trough.

ANGRY FARMER: Who raided my vegetable
                patch?
NOT-SO-INNOCENT PIG: Beets me!

Why are pigs such early risers?
Did you ever try to shut off a rooster?

Do pigs like Backgammon?
No, they prefer their backs scratched.

What happened to the little pig who wore green socks to school?
She didn't get pinched on St. Patrick's Day.

Mama Pig has a great, new kitchen appliance that lets her prepare meals ahead. It's called a garbage compactor.

I hear the pigs have put in a snack bar.
Yes, it's a long plank covered with fly paper.

What do you get when you cross a pig with
an elephant?
A very large animal that knows a lot of jokes.

HOGGISCOPE

ARIES pigs are natural leaders who enjoy barnyard politics — it lets them do a lot of mudslinging.

Practical TAURUS wants all the lady pigs to run on a tread mill so the farm can convert to SOW-ler power.

Fast-talking GEMINI gets more than his share of the slop, causing the others to squeal on him, but he doesn't mind. This pig's motto is, "All's well that ends swill."

Cautious CANCER doesn't want to hear of a handsome stranger in her future. She's afraid he'll turn out to be a ranch butcher.

Proud LEO doesn't have just a mudhole — he has a mudfilled hot-tub, complete to swill cooler and quadraphonic hog calls.

Sty-lish VIRGO worries that the pigs will smell when visitors call — so she's trying to get all the pigs to wear clothespins on their noses.

The LIBRA pigs are so social-minded, they've founded the first barnyard branch of the SPCA (Sows Preventing Chicken Administration).

The SCORPIO pig is out for blood — wolf's blood. This daring pig has heard all Mother Goose's shoat tales and wants revenge!

Adventure-loving SAGITTARIUS means to run away with the circus, so he can travel with the pig-top and try to hit the pig time.

Practical CAPRICORN does her Christmas slopping by mail. She knows the streets are so full of road hogs, it's impossible to find porking space.

The free-spirited AQUARIUS pig has made her family very oinxious. She says she feels sorry for that poor unloved wolf and has invited him to dinner.

Gentle PISCES would like to hold a garden party, but she's afraid her friends will embarass her by making complete hogs of themselves.

HOW DO YOU RECOGNIZE A TEXAS PIG?
It will eat anything, but prefers baked Alaska.
It's the one with the real cowboy boots.
Instead of finding truffles, it sniffs out oil wells.

HOW CAN YOU TELL A CALIFORNIA PIG?
It's the one who demands Perrier with its swill.
It has a hot tub instead of a mudhole.
It's the one with the feathered hatband.

CUSTOMER AT SODA FOUNTAIN: Can you make a pig cooler?
WAITER: Sure, spray him with a hose.
CUSTOMER: Can you make a pig shake?
WAITER: Tell him the wolf is coming.
CUSTOMER: How do you make a pig float?
WAITER: Just give him an inner tube.

All the pigs are crazy over a new horror movie about a giant hog that paddles around in the surf biting swimmers. It's called "Jowls!"

What do you call an oversize motorcycle for pigs?
A hog hog.

What do you call a pig in a steel foundry?
A pig pig.

MAMA SOW: Would you like a nice cake with three candles for your party?
GREEDY PIGLET: I'd rather have three cakes and one candle.

Why won't the witch let the traveling pig actors into her gingerbread cottage?
She's afraid they'll bring down the house.

How can you recognize a Gnome Pig?
They're the ones with the little red hats.

Tom Swifties

"I didn't save any leftovers for the hogs," Tom said piggishly.

"I don't think much of your new boy pig," Tom said boarishly.

"That hog's too small," Tom said shoatly.

"I let the girl pig loose," Tom said swine-ily.